MW00960659

Ever
Quiz Book

101 Questions That Will Test Your Knowledge of This Prestigious Club

Published by Glowworm Press
7 Nuffield Way
Abingdon OX14 1RL

By Chris Carpenter

Everton Football Club

This Everton Football Club quiz book contains one hundred and one informative and entertaining trivia questions with multiple choice answers. Some of the questions are easy, yet most are quite challenging, and this book is guaranteed to test your knowledge and memory of the club's long and successful history.

You will be quizzed on players, legends, managers, opponents, transfer deals, trophies, records, honours, fixtures, terrace songs and much more, guaranteeing you an educational experience and hours of fun. Informative, enjoyable and fun, this Everton FC Quiz Book will provide the ultimate in entertainment for all Evertonians, and will test your knowledge of **Everton Football Club** and prove you know the club's history.

Disclaimer

Let's start with some relatively easy questions.

1. When was Everton founded?
   A. 1872
   B. 1876
   C. 1878

2. What is Everton's nickname?
   A. The Candies
   B. The Sweeties
   C. The Toffees

3. Where do Everton play their home games?
   A. Stadium of Light
   B. Goodison Park
   C. White Hart Lane

4. What is the stadium's capacity?
   A. 39,572
   B. 38,257
   C. 37,725

5. Who or what is the club mascot?
   A. Changy the Elephant
   B. Captain Canary
   C. Toffee The Tiger

6. Who has made the most appearances for the club in total?
   A. Brian Labone
   B. Ted Sagar
   C. Neville Southall

7. Who is the club's record goal scorer?
   A. Dixie Dean
   B. Graeme Sharp
   C. Joe Royle

8. Which Everton striker holds the record for the fastest ever goal scored in an FA Cup Final?
   A. Tim Cahill
   B. Louis Saha

C. Victor Anichebe

9. Which of the following song do the players run out to?
    A. Theme Tune to The Sweeney
    B. Theme Tune To Dr Who
    C. Theme Tune to Z Cars

10. Which of these is a well known pub near the ground?
    A. The Winding Road
    B. The Wine Cellar
    C. The Winslow

OK, so here are the answers to the first ten questions. If you get eight or more right, you are doing well but the questions will get harder.

A1. Everton was founded in 1878.

A2. Everton's nickname is of course the Toffees.

A3. Everton play their home games at Goodison Park.

A4. The current stadium capacity is 39,572.

A5. The club mascot is Changy the Elephant.

A6. Neville Southall has made the most appearances for the club. He played in 750 first-team matches between 1981 and 1998. Legend.

A7. Dixie Dean is Everton's record goal scorer with 383 goals in all competitions.

A8. Louis Saha holds the record for the fastest goal recorded in an FA Cup Final scoring after 25 seconds against Chelsea at Wembley in May 2009.

A9. The players run out to the theme tune to the 1960s TV series 'Z Cars'.

A10. The Winslow is a well known pub near the ground. Be prepared to queue for a pint though.

OK, back to the questions.

11. What is the highest number of goals that Everton has scored in a league season?
    A. 109
    B. 115
    C. 121

12. What is the fewest number of goals that Everton has conceded in a league season?
    A. 25
    B. 27
    C. 29

13. Who has scored the most penalties for the club?
    A. Leighton Baines
    B. Roy Vernon
    C. David Unsworth

14. Who has made the most league appearances for the club?
    A. Howard Kendall
    B. Brian Labone
    C. Neville Southall

15. What is the home end of the ground known as?
    A. Bullens Road
    B. Gwladys Street Stand
    C. Park End Stand

16. What is the club's record attendance?
    A. 74,992
    B. 76,929
    C. 78,299

17. Where is Everton's training ground?
    A. Finch Farm
    B. Robin Farm
    C. Thrush Farm

18. What is the name of the road the ground is on?
    A. Millennium Way

B. Goodison Road
C. Newcastle Road

19. Which stand has the biggest capacity?
    A. The Bullens Road Stand
    B. The Park End Stand
    C. The Goodison Road Stand

20. What is the size of the pitch?
    A. 112x72 yards
    B. 105x68 yards
    C. 105x62 yards

Here are the answers to the last set of questions.

A11. Everton scored an incredible 121 goals in 42 matches in the Second Division in the season of 1930/31, which is the highest for the club.

A12. Everton conceded just 27 goals in 40 matches in the First Division in the season of 1987/88, which is the least for the club.

A13. David Unsworth has scored the most penalties for the club, scoring a total of 23 out of 25, not a bad record.

A14. Neville Southall, with 578 league appearances holds the record for the most league appearances for the club.

A15. The home end of the ground is Gwladys Street Stand, sometimes better known as 'The Street End'.

A16. Everton's record home attendance is 78,299 against Liverpool on 18th September 1933.

A17. Everton's training ground is located in Finch Farm.

A18. Goodison Road is the name of the road the ground is on.

A19. The Goodison Road Stand has the largest capacity, being able to accommodate 12,664 people.

A20. The size of the pitch is 112 yards long by 72 yards wide. By way of comparison, Wembley's pitch is 115 yards long by 75 yards wide

Now we move onto some questions about the club's records.

21. What is the club's record win in any competition?
        A. 10-2
        B. 11-2
        C. 12-2

22. Who did they beat?
        A. Fairfield
        B. Derby County
        C. Stockport County

23. In which season?
        A. 1889/90
        B. 1901/02
        C. 1909/10

24. What is the club's record win in the league?
        A. 8-0
        B. 9-1
        C. 10-2

25. Who did they beat?
        A. Coventry City
        B. Manchester City
        C. Plymouth Argyle

26. What is the club's record *away* win in the league?
        A. 5-0
        B. 6-0
        C. 7-0

27. What is the club's record defeat?
        A. 0-7
        B. 1-8
        C. 1-9

28. Who against?
        A. Arsenal
        B. Sunderland
        C. Wolverhampton Wanderers

29. In Everton's title winning season of 1927/28, how many
    League goals did Dixie Dean score?
    A. 40
    B. 50
    C. 60

30. Who has scored the most hat tricks for Everton?
    A. Tony Cottee
    B. Dixie Dean
    C. Graeme Sharp

Here are the answers to the last set of questions.

A21. The club's record win in any competition is 11-2.

A22. Everton beat Derby County 11-2 in the Fifth round of FA Cup with hat tricks from Fred Geary, Alec Brady and Alf Milward.

A23. The match took place on 18th January 1890, so it is the 1889/90 season.

A24. The club's record win in the League is 9-1.

A25. The 9-1 record margin has been recorded twice - against Manchester City on 3rd September 1906 and Plymouth Argyle on 27th December 1930. Give yourself a bonus point if you knew that.

A26. The club's record away win in the League is a 7-0 victory at Charlton Athletic on 7th February 1931.

A27. The club's record defeat in any competition is 0-7.

A28. All three clubs have beaten Everton 7-0, with the defeat at Arsenal in May 2005 being the most recent

A29. Dixie Dean scored a staggering 60 league goals in the title winning season. It was a record in this country at the time, and remains a record, and almost certainly will never be broken.

A30. Dixie Dean scored 37 hat tricks, which is the highest for the club. Dixie was a true legend.

Now we move onto questions about the club's trophies.

31. When did the club win their first league title?
    A. 1890/91
    B. 1894/95
    C. 1898/99

32. When did the club win their first FA Cup?
    A. 1886
    B. 1896
    C. 1906

33. Who did they beat in the final?
    A. Ipswich Town
    B. Sunderland
    C. Newcastle United

34. What was the score?
    A. 1-0
    B. 2-1
    C. 4-1

35. How many times have Everton won the League?
    A. 5
    B. 7
    C. 9

36. How many times have Everton won the FA Cup?
    A. 4
    B. 5
    C. 6

37. How many times have the club won the League Cup?
    A. 0
    B. 1
    C. 2

38. Who was the last captain to lift the League trophy?
    A. Howard Kendall
    B. Kevin Ratcliffe
    C. Peter Reid

39. Who was the last captain to lift the FA Cup?
   A. Neville Southall
   B. Dave Watson
   C. Barry Horne

40. Who was captain in the club's last appearance in the League Cup Final?
   A. Alan Irvine
   B. Graeme Sharp
   C. Kevin Ratcliffe

Here are your answers to the last ten questions.

A31. Everton won their first league title in 1890/91.

A32. Everton won their first FA Cup on the 21st April 1906.

A33. Everton defeated Newcastle United at Crystal Palace in the 1906 FA Cup final held at the Crystal Palace Sports Centre.

A34. Everton won 1-0, with a goal from Alex "Sandy" Young.

A35. Everton have won the League 9 times in total.

A36. Everton have won the FA Cup 5 times.

A37. Everton have never won the League Cup. However they have been finalists in 1977 and 1984.

A38. Kevin Ratcliffe was the last captain to lift the League trophy at the end of the 1986/87 season.

A39. Dave Watson was the last captain to lift the FA Cup. He lifted the cup when Everton defeated Manchester United 1-0 on 20th May 1995.

A40. Kevin Ratcliffe was the captain in the club's last League Cup Final. He skippered the side when Everton lost 1-0 to Liverpool in 1984.

I hope you're getting most of the answers right.

41. What is the record transfer fee paid?
    A. £28 million
    B. £30 million
    C. £32 million

42. Who was the record transfer fee paid for?
    A. Romelu Lukaku
    B. Jordan Pickford
    C. Gylfi Sigurdsson

43. What is the record transfer fee received?
    A. £55 million
    B. £65 million
    C. £75 million

44. Who was the record transfer fee received for?
    A. Marouane Fellaini
    B. Romelu Lukaku
    C. John Stones

45. Who was the first Everton player to play for England?
    A. Alf Milward
    B. Johnny Holt
    C. Fred Geary

46. Who has won the most international caps whilst an Everton player?
    A. Neville Southall
    B. Kevin Ratcliffe
    C. Tim Cahill

47. Who has scored the most international goals whilst at Everton?
    A. William Dean and Gary Lineker
    B. Tim Cahill and Gary Lineker
    C. Tim Cahill and William Dean

48. Who is the youngest player ever to represent the club?
    A. Dave Watson
    B. Jake Bidwell

C. Jose Baxter

49. Who is the youngest ever goal scorer?
    A. A McKinnon
    B. James Vaughan
    C. Bob Latchford

50. Who is the oldest player ever to represent the club?
    A. Neville Southall
    B. Jose Baxter
    C. Ted Sagar

Here is the latest set of answers.

A41. Everton paid £45 million for an Icelandic footballer, which is their record transfer.

A42. The record transfer fee is £45 million which the club paid to Swansea City for Gylfi Sigurdsson on 16th August 2017.

A43. The record transfer fee received by Everton is £75 million.

A44. The fee was received from Manchester City for Romelu Lukaku in August 2017. It is a healthy profit on a player that was bought for £28 million from Chelsea in 2014.

A45. Johnny Holt was the first Everton player to play for England.

A46. Neville Southall won 91 caps for the Wales while he was at Everton, which is the highest for the club.

A47. Tim Cahill and William Dean scored 18 international goals each whilst Everton players.

A48. Jose Baxter is the youngest player ever to represent the club. He made his first team debut at the age of 16 years, 191 days against Blackburn Rovers on 16th August 2008.

A49. James Vaughn is the youngest ever goal scorer for Everton. He scored against Crystal Palace aged 16 years and 271 days on 10th April 2005.

A50. Ted Sagar is the oldest player ever to represent the club. He appeared for the club against Plymouth Argyle on 15th November 1952 at the age of 42 years and 281 days.

I hope you're learning some new facts about the club. Onto the next set of questions.

51. Who is Everton's oldest ever goal scorer?
    A. Walter Fielding
    B. Jack Taylor
    C. Mark Hughes

52. Who is the club's longest serving manager of all time?
    A. Howard Kendall
    B. David Moyes
    C. Thomas McIntosh

53. Who is the club's longest serving post war manager?
    A. Ian Buchan
    B. Harry Catterick
    C. Gordon Lee

54. What is the name of the Everton match day programme?
    A. Everton official matchday programme
    B. Everton Diaries
    C. Official Toffees Programme

55. How many times did David Moyes win LMA Manager of the Year?
    A. 1
    B. 2
    C. 3

56. Which of these is an Everton fanzine?
    A. Everton Diaries
    B. When Skies are Grey
    C. Not the view

57. What motif is on the club crest?
    A. A beehive
    B. A tower
    C. A windmill

58. What is the club's motto?
    A. Consectatio Excellentiae
    B. Labor omnia vincit

C. Nil Satis Nisi Optimum

59. Who is considered as Everton's main rivals?
    A. Accrington Stanley
    B. Liverpool
    C. Tranmere Rovers

60. What could be regarded as the club's most well known chant?
    A. Blue is The Colour
    B. Royal Blue Mersey
    C. The Blaydon Races

Here are the answers to the last set of questions.

A51. Walter Fielding is Everton's oldest ever goal scorer. He scored against West Bromwich Albion at the age of 38 years and 305 days.

A52. Thomas McIntosh is the club's longest serving manager of all time. He served from 1919-35 and managed 719 matches.

A53. Harry Catterick is the club's longest serving post war manager. He served from 1961-73 managing a total of 594 matches.

A54. The catchy name of the Everton match day programme is 'Everton official matchday programme'.

A55. David Moyes won the award three times; only Sir Alex Ferguson has won it more times.

A56. When Skies are Grey is perhaps the best known of the Everton fanzines.

A57. Everton's badge consists of Prince Rupert's tower. The tower has been inextricably linked with the Everton area since its construction in 1787. It still stands today on Everton Brow in Netherfield Road.

A58.The Latin motto of Everton is 'Nil Satis, Nisi Optimum'. It means 'Nothing but the best is good enough' in English.

A59. Liverpool is of course Everton's main rival.

A60. 'Royal Blue Mersey' can be regarded as the club's most well known chant.

Let's give you some easier questions.

61. What is the traditional colour of the home shirt?
    A. Royal blue
    B. Red
    C. Green

62. What is the traditional colour of the away shirt?
    A. White
    B. Yellow and green stripes
    C. Red

63. Who is the current club sponsor?
    A. Bidvest
    B. Chang
    C. SportPesa

64. Who was the first club shirt sponsor?
    A. Boylesports
    B. Danka
    C. Hafnia

65. Which of these sports brands has not supplied kit to Everton?
    A. Adidas
    B. Umbro
    C. Le Coq Sportif

66. Who is currently the club chairman?
    A. Bill Kenwright
    B. Robert Elstone
    C. David Miliband

67. Who was the club's first foreign signing?
    A. Dan Doyle
    B. Jacob Lewin
    C. Bob Kelso

68. Who was the club's first black player?
    A. Tony McNamara
    B. Cliff Marshall
    C. Andy Rankin

69. Who was the club's first match in the league against?
     A. Accrington Stanley
     B. Blackburn Rovers
     C. Bolton Wanderers

70. Who won the player of the year award for the 2017/18 season?
     A. Tom Davies
     B. Phil Jagielka
     C. Jordan Pickford

Here are the answers to the last set of questions.

A61. The traditional colour of the home shirt is of course royal blue.

A62. The traditional colour of the away shirt is white.

A63. SportPesa is the current shirt sponsor. They are a Kenyan sports betting platform who took over from long term sponsor Chang Beer before the start of the 2017/18 season.

A64. Hafnia was the first shirt sponsor of Everton, first sponsoring the shirts back in 1979.

A65. Adidas has never supplied kit to Everton whereas Le Coq Sportif and Umbro have.

A66. Bill Kenwright is the current club chairman.

A67. Jacob Lewin was the club's first foreign signing.

A68. Cliff Marshall was the club's first black player.

A69. The club's first match in the league was against Accrington Stanley which was played on 8th September 1888 with Everton winning the match 2-1.

A70. Goalkeeper Jordan Pickford won the 2017/18 player of the season award.

Here is the next batch of ten carefully chosen questions

71. Who was the first ever double hat trick scorer for Everton?
    A. Dixie Dean
    B. Fred Geary
    C. Jack Southworth

72. Which of these brands is the current kit manufacturer?
    A. Nike
    B. Umbro
    C. Puma

73. Which Scottish forward was nicknamed "The Golden Ghost"?
    A. Andy Gray
    B. Graeme Sharp
    C. Alex Young

74. Who holds the record for the most clean-sheets for the club?
    A. Tim Howard
    B. Neville Southall
    C. Ted Sagar

75. What position did the club finish at the end of the 2017/18 season?
    A. 6th
    B. 7th
    C. 8th

76. Who was the first manager of the club?
    A. Theo Kelly
    B. Will Cuff
    C. W.C Barclay

77. What was the transfer fee paid for Jordan Pickford by the club?
    A. £23 million
    B. £25 million
    C. £27 million

78. How many FA Cup goals did Dixie Dean score for the club?
   - A. 20
   - B. 28
   - C. 33

79. Which of these played in goal for Everton?
   - A. Neville Chamberlain
   - B. Neville Southall
   - C. Nicky Southall

80. Who owns the club?
   - A. John Henry
   - B. Bill Kenwright
   - C. Farhad Moshari

Here are the answers to the last ten questions.

A71. Jack Southworth was the first ever double hat trick scorer of Everton.

A72. Umbro is the current Everton kit manufacturer.

A73. Alex Young was nicknamed "The Golden Ghost".

A74. With 269 clean-sheets, Neville Southall holds the record for the most clean-sheets for the club

A75. Everton finished the 2017/18 season in a respectable 8th position.

A76. W.C Barclay was the first full time manager of the club. He managed the club from August 1888 to May 1889.

A77. £25 million was paid to Sunderland for Jordan Pickford in June 2017, with the possibility of it rising to £30 million in add-ons

A78. Of course it is Everton legend Neville Southall who played in goal for the club for 17 years.

A79. Jimmy Harris was the first League Cup goal scorer for the club.

A80. Iranian billionaire Moshari bought the club in February 2016.

Here are the next set of questions, let's hope you get most of them right.

81. Who has made the most appearances as a substitute for the club?
    A. Jack Taylor
    B. Mick Lyons
    C. Victor Anichebe

82. What shirt number does Theo Walcott wear?
    A. 11
    B. 14
    C. 17

83. Who was the first Everton player to win the PFA Players' Player of the Year Award?
    A. Peter Reid
    B. Gary Lineker
    C. Tim Cahill

84. When did Everton win their only European Cup Winners' Cup?
    A. 1974
    B. 1980
    C. 1985

85. Who did they beat in the final of the European Cup Winners' Cup?
    A. Rapid Vienna
    B. Inter Milan
    C. Real Madrid

86. Why are Everton called the Toffees?
    A. The ground was near a toffee factory
    B. The ground was near a toffee shop
    C. Owners nick name was toffee

87. Who has scored the highest number of goals in a season for the club?
    A. Graeme Sharp
    B. Bob Latchford
    C. Dixie Dean

88. What shirt number does Tom Davies wear?
   A. 16
   B. 26
   C. 36

89. Who or what was nicknamed 'The Grand Old Lady'?
   A. Andy Gray
   B. Goodison Park
   C. Stanley Park

90. Who is considered as Everton's greatest manager of all time?
   A. Ian Buchan
   B. Howard Kendall
   C. David Moyes

Here are the answers to the last block of questions.

A81. Victor Anichebe has made the most appearances as a substitute for the club

A82. Theo Walcott wears shirt number 11.

A83. Peter Reid the first Everton player to win the PFA Players' Player of the Year Award. He won the award for his efforts during the 1984/85 season.

A84. Everton won their only European Cup Winners' Cup in 1985.

A85. Everton defeated Rapid Vienna 3-1 in the final in Rotterdam on 15th May 1985 with the goals being scored by Andy Gray, Trevor Steven and Kevin Sheedy.

A86. Everton are known as the Toffees because the ground was near a toffee shop, famous for selling an Everton Mint.

A87. Dixie Dean scored 60 goals in the 1927/28 season, which is the highest number of goals ever scored in a season for the club.

A88. Tom Davies currently wears shirt number 26.

A89. Goodison Park is nicknamed 'The Grand Old Lady". It is not as complimentary as you may think though. In 1999, a piece in the Independent newspaper went as follows... "Another potential suitor has apparently thought better of Everton, walking away on Tuesday from the sagging Grand Old Lady of English football, leaving her still in desperate need of a makeover".

A90. Howard Kendall is widely regarded as the most successful manager in the history of Everton.

Here is the final set of questions. Enjoy!

91. When were Everton relegated to the Second Division for the first time?
    A. 1902/03
    B. 1928/29
    C. 1930/31

92. Who scored a brace in the 1966 FA Cup final win?
    A. Derek Temple
    B. Ray Wilson
    C. Mike Trebilcock

93. Who is the highest goal scorer for the club in the *Premier League era*?
    A. Mikel Arteta
    B. Tim Cahill
    C. Duncan Ferguson

94. What nationality is Morgan Schneiderlin?
    A. Dutch
    B. French
    C. German

95. Who was nicknamed "The Little General"?
    A. Peter Reid
    B. Bobby Collins
    C. Jimmy Harris

96. Who scored the winning goal in the 1995 FA Cup final against Manchester United?
    A. Barry Horne
    B. Graham Stuart
    C. Paul Rideout

97. Which of the following is a popular Everton chant?
    A. All together now
    B. We don't care
    C. Gone with the wind

98. In which season did Everton last win the League?
    A. 1969/70

B. 1984/85
C. 1986/87

99. How many appearances did Ted Sagar make for the club?
    A. 500
    B. 514
    C. 517

100.What number shirt does Leighton Baines wear?
    A. 3
    B. 13
    C. 23

101.Whose statue is present outside Goodison Park?
    A. Dixie Dean
    B. Howard Kendall
    C. Graeme Sharp

Here goes with the last set of answers.

A91. Everton was relegated to the Second Division for the first time in the season of 1930-31.

A92. Mike Trebilcock scored a brace in the 1966 FA Cup final win against Sheffield Wednesday.

A93. With 60 Premier League goals, Duncan Ferguson is the highest goal scorer for the club in the Premier League era.

A94. Morgan Schneiderlin is French.

A95. Bobby Collins was nicknamed "The Little General".

A96. Paul Rideout scored the only goal of the game in the 1995 FA Cup final against Manchester United. It was a headed goal in the 30th minute after a Graham Stuart shot had rebounded off the crossbar.

A97. "All together now" is a popular Everton chant.

A98. The last time Everton won the league was in the 1986/87 season.

A99. Ted Sagar made 500 appearances for the club.

A100. Left back Baines wears shirt number 3.

A101. A stunning statue of Dixie Dean stands proudly on Walton Lane just outside Goodison Park. It was unveiled in May 2001.

That's it. I hope you enjoyed this ebook, and I hope you got most of the answers right. I also hope you learnt one or two new things about the club.

Thanks for reading, and showing your support for this historic club. Please be so kind as to leave a positive review on Amazon.

Printed in Great Britain
by Amazon